Scotia Nova

Scotia Nova

Poems for the Early Days
of a Better Nation

Edited by ALISTAIR FINDLAY
and TESSA RANSFORD

Luath Press Limited
EDINBURGH
www.luath.co.uk

First published 2014

ISBN: 978-1-910021-10-1

The publishers acknowledge the support of

ALBA | CHRUTHACHAIL

towards the publication of this volume.

The paper used in this book is recyclable. It is made from
low chlorine pulps produced in a low energy, low emissions
manner from renewable forests.

Printed and bound by
Bell & Bain Ltd., Glasgow

Typeset in 11 point Sabon
by 3btype.com

Contents

Preface

ALTHOUGH THE IDEA of this anthology was first mooted in August 2013, the process of calling for submissions did not begin until January 2014 with a deadline for the end of March. Publisher and editors agreed that for practical purposes we should pitch our requests to all authors published by Luath, a considerable number of writers, plus selected poets often chosen to ensure that the anthology would meet the diversity and inclusiveness that its theme envisaged. The call for submissions spelled out the breadth of concerns we hoped contributors might wish to respond to through the medium of poetry:

> Whatever the outcome of Scotland's Independence Referendum on 18 September 2014, a better Scotland is possible. Across every aspect of life in Scotland – housing inequality, life expectancy, health, education, crime, sectarianism, localism and more – we all know that a better Scotland is possible. And then there is Trident. And the Bedroom Tax. And the Democratic Deficit. And on and on it goes.

Readers will judge for themselves as to how well this brief has been fulfilled, but the editors are certainly delighted with the quality as well as the variety of response. There are no poems explicitly titled 'Trident' or 'The Bedroom Tax' and so on, but the arguments informing these issues and all the others suggested, colour many of the poems included. There are poems dealing with the 'politics' of the Referendum itself, as might be expected, but also poems dealing with a range of literary, social, cultural, identity, historical, personal, trans-cultural, inter-generational, religious and spiritual subject-matters, sufficiently thought-provoking to us as poets and editors. As a glimpse of what a slice of Scotland's contemporary poets and writers are feeling about the place in which we live and breathe and work today, we hope readers will feel as vitalised as we have been in the course of editing this anthology. Our thanks go to all the contributors.

All the poems have been written or adapted for this anthology save the opening one by Angus Calder who, had he still been with us, would undoubtedly have contributed to it, indeed, may well have co-edited it, and been as enthused as ourselves in the process. A radical cultural historian, literary scholar and poet, Angus was one of the moving forces behind the formation of the Scottish Poetry Library. His poem on the gulls, pigeons and sparrows of Scotland, flocking round Holyrood's Palace, Parliament and Poetry Library, is as much about the varieties of human being and the competing 'tribes' that comprise modern Scotland as it is about the 'gulls' and 'nature' that he insists (too much perhaps!) is his only interest. The poem's theme – the constant remaking of contemporary Scotland – embraces all the poems in this anthology, while Michael Knowles' cover photograph, of a gull standing on an eagle's head at the base of Henry Dundas' statue in St Andrew's Square (emblem of Scotland's centuries long ties to Old Corruption and Imperial Rule), portrays the same message visually, of something quite different emerging. We commend all to you.

Alistair Findlay
Tessa Ransford

Talking to Mario Relich about Gulls in Edinburgh

Angus Calder

The pigeons and gulls have taken over the town.
They are nesting here now (the gulls, I mean.)
The pigeons command all pavements, with their low brows
and determined strut, the boldest you've ever seen.
I like pigeons and gulls because they confirm
that life never stops changing. The scene
has been transformed by the pigeons and gulls
quite recently, taking over from the sparrows.
Nostalgic persons might talk as if life has been narrowed,
but I love the gulls, and the pigeons. They express
'nature' at its worst and its damned best,
refusing to stop pecking, refusing to die,
always prepared to give it another try
and (gulls, I mean) flying upwards towards the sun.

In Thir Haunds

Donald Adamson

Afore the present chynges tae
an echo doon ma mind's
tuim corridors and fades awaa,
afore Ah'm blotted oot
bi the muckle snaa
wi white feathers whisperin
'Wheesht' and 'Sleep'
Ah want tae say

that Ah wis born in this land
and Ah'll maist likely dee here
and Ah hae a dream o a future
abuin the oozie, glaurie tides o hate,
the chaunts, the threits, the marchin bands, parades,
the drums duntit, tubs thumpit –

Wha's like us? fowk blaw
but Ah ask masell:
Wha'll dae better than us?
And Ah hope the answer's wi us, in oor bairns
and oor bairns' bairns,
blatterin doon the waas o prejudice,
openin thir minds, airms, herts
tae brithers, sisters, kent or unkent, aa.

Kirkaig Falls

Jim Aitken

Mountain and loch, river and stream
All painted in purple and green;
Heather and fern, rock and tree
Ancient and modern and free.

Water plunges brown with peat
Like a torrent of Highland malt;
Wind and rain and spume blend
And sharpen the senses like ice.

A fiery cocktail rages through the glen
Going where it has to go;
Deadlines to meet with the sea
Have been kept for thousands of years.

The sky darkens and birds vanish.
In among the trees and bracken,
The rocks and the stones,
Moss and grass and bog,
Silence lies hidden under thick cloud.

But our high-dive expert
Somersaults and leaps
Just as before
For in him runs the blood
Of the country that bred him.

On Top

Pamela Beasant

If Scotland is a body
I live in one of the wee hats
on top.

Scotland sometimes forgets it's wearing hats.

On maps, it sometimes
takes them off,
or tucks them under an arm.

If it's not careful,
the wee hats might one day
blow clean away,

and Scotland will be a bit
chilly round the lugs,
unadorned.

Citizens' Song

David Betteridge

We are the V at the ship's prow,
    the thrust of the engine,
        and its turning screw;
    we are the voyage, and its hazards,
and the landfall we pursue.

We are the loom, the shuttle, and the cloth,
    the thread, the needle,
        and the tailor's care;
    we are the wearer's nakedness,
and the garments that are ours to wear.

We are the smith, the hammer,
    and the anvilled metal that we beat;
        we are the fashioned artefact,
    well-tempered
in our forge's heat.

We are the grit that seeds the pearl,
    the nutrient tide, and the oyster-bed;
        we are our land's harvest, gathered
    and golden,
and, each day, the risen bread.

Beaten

Hazel Buchan Cameron

We squabble across burnt heather and walk the butt path
where frozen starlight rests; sequins over tweedy ground.
When we stop at a cairn for breath, we notice a man
    further on,
his shooting bunnet drawn half-over his eyes, arms down,
each shoulder drooped by the weight of a double brace –
each grouse still beautiful but sinking down in its skin,
ready to be hung. He hardly raises an eyebrow as we pass –
ignores my greeting. When we reach the final butt, he's gone.
I see no way forward; then remember *the season* is over.

A Wee Word of Advice from the Empire

Ken Cockburn

It's not difficult.

Listen. You worship
who you like BUT
the Emperor's a god
AND I want the taxes in
by the new moon.

All right?
If it's not
it won't be just me
and Valerius here
come next time.

Celtic disaggregation

Des Dillon

In the hangover from Scotland's greatest
glorious defeat, retribution swarms
north from the halls of the tender south.
Day did not break well on the whisky song
we sang: This land is your land, this land
is my land, from the Whithorn Irish, to the
Shetland Vikings, from the Gaels of Tiree,
to the oil rich north sea, this land was made

for you and me. On the count our nerve failed
The day forever gone, our future nailed.
Snakes in whisper slither from every nook
and cranny and we canny dae a hing
but sing, lament, witness, this final
disaggregation of our nation.

Thir Meters Yit are Current Quha Will Leuk

Colin Donati

Ae Winter nicht, as I brocht hame on fute
in twa Tesco bags throu the ice sum fare,
it clecked in mind, I ken no on what wit,
hou that ae friend, near seivin year or mair
by me nor seen nor kend whair that he were,
maun leive yet, blythe; dree what he wad, fare furth;
in peace or pyne, be traikin roun this ëarth.

Aneath yon mune hou mony million folk!
and yet, frae aa the thrangity, fell few
loued or bidden wi in special; as, in yoke,
haein little aucht oorsels, we warsle throu,
tak pairtners gin we can, for fear pit to,
aye lippenin ilk ane ane upo anither –
to think on it pits Gode ein in a swither.

Sen at the college, blate-kind, saikless, puir,
I leuk't on unkent authors to win leir
(sma heed gin they, as me, scant be as shair
anent the workings o God's warld, for weer)
the auld Scots Makars I wis niver sweer
to read in, takkin pleisance in their thocht,
kythe wi the leid they tret wi echt or ocht.

And Henrysoun was aye and frae the first
the ane I clicked wi, albeid I wes dull
and didna hear the hauf o what was hirst
intil his lines, for lack o guide, and full
mony times I made retour to mull
owre his few pages thinkan *here* was grain
yet tellan nocht the starn corn there, but pain.

Full queer it is to think hou it gaes back
guid fower, five, or mair sax-hunner year
sen that this man on yird drew braith and spak;
and wonder mair his words ring nou als clear
as ony leid the day in mensefu ear:
his tung, tho bye, maun bide a wee but dout,
gin's seids in sic fail grund as mines can root.

For quhy the mair I think on Henrysoun,
(thocht he be but in prent) the mair I see
as canny, wyce and fair humane a man
as eir had feel and hairt for poetry;
oor side o time, kent aa tholes sair in fee,
yet didna aye juist haud wi upcasts dour,
nor gustless frïars scauls, sae snip, sae sour.

And as it cam, sen I wes thinkand this,
that in aa Scotland there's but few taks tent
for sair (and sic as dae, maist say nae miss
comes be negleck, sen nocht is modren in't)
gie leave to me to demonstrate a point:
mak choice frae out his poems and compair
until the case the day and see quhat were.

In *Cresseid* of 'Pole Artik' maks he mention:
the haill *Antartik* photographed frae space
is on my hall door принд up for attention
(cut frae ane Scotsman airticle nae less)
to fleg the reader (wi nae fenyeit case?)
hou Ice Sheet Larsen B, were it to brak,
wad queel the Gulf Stream and gie Europe wrack

That's some year bye; nae dout but nou it's dune;
we're still here, and *the wedder* nae thing constant
but in *in*constancy – whilk Henrysoun
wad fain be first to recognise, but dant,
wi aa his *schouris off hail* that he micht scant
frae cauld *defend* himsel. And sae wi us,
for aa oor nuclear chaffers infamous.

Syne wes I readan Eliot's *Fower Quartets*:
the openin tae the *Preachin o the Swallow*
scarce taks nae less a sklent askance, wi its
cosmic mints at God. As for *the hollow
men, the stuffed men lent thegither*, altho
the comparisoun is nae thing parfit,
the Fox, the Wolff, the Cok, aa kinna fit.

Yet why am I nou thinkand in this wise?
quhat thir twae cheils to me are is past wit
(gin o the sowl a body can hae prise
that mortal is, it's no frae *thinkan* on it)
the tane a makar, kent but frae his dit;
the tither, tint freind sumtyme tae me kent
frae coontless ither quaintance til us sent.

Wi cairriers in haun, as I heretofore sayn,
I turnt in fro the street an tuke the stair,
sclimmed up thae flichts to quhaur, aa be its lane,
my stairheid dwellan wes (leuk gin ye care)
that wi a puckle weill kent strangers share;
fair taffled, tirl't the key in lock and fure,
howpan for lissance, in and throw the dure

Moralitas

The secret for to crack sic keys to leid
as Scots or ochtlike, gin ye seek the knit,
is in the soun; to teachers pey nae heed
that tell ye ithergaits – a bairn wad ken it –
nae hairm tae tak a dictionar for wit,
yit mind an seek the soun o't gin ye can,
the soond is aa, an aa thing follaes than.

In the Wind Country

Morgan Downie

what it is to live
in the wind country,
a land that is not home
unless staked down,
battened, secure
under lash.
to fight and curse,
to struggle until
finally, only to thole.

the wind restless, snaps
at slate, vain shutters.
a door slams back and forth,
first light, then not.

to be at the shore
where the incoming waves
shriek at the air like the wail
of sea-buried sailors.

on the breezed lea of the dune
the sundial geometric
of the single bladed grass
dials the image of the sun.

the wind is cruel here
filled with the loon
song of seals
a northern emptiness
tonguing the ear
with the voices
of the dead.
furious life,
without end.

The West Lothian Question Answered (i.m. Margo MacDonald)

Alistair Findlay

I remember asking my father long ago, TV screen
    flickering in monochrome,
slumped in the big chair watching the by-election,
    a Labour man,
through and through, Tam Dalyell's staunchest ally,
    yet fair to Billy Wolfe
as well, in the pages of the local paper he wrote for,
    The West Lothian Courier,
this very question: what did he think of big Margo,
    a once blonde
and busty barmaid, he paused a mo', *a formidable
opponent*
in a stair-heid row, he declared, without looking
    up, but he knew,
as we all knew soon enough, she was much more
    than this,
a champion of the people, doughty and true, a
    fighter for the cause.

And now she's gone, but I can see her, strapped
    like Kate Winslet
to the prow of yon converted aircraft carrier,
    The Robert Burns,
the hospital ship her husband Jim wants sent
    round the world,

on international rescue missions, delivering
    human aid wherever
natural disasters occur, crewed by young Scots,
    voluntary service overseas,
a new form o' globalisation, and see, there
    she is, boldly looking out,
The Proclaimers roaring Celine Dion's soaring,
    song, and my old man
lookin' down an' bellowin' – *Gaun, Margo!*
    Gaun!

Sonnet 18914

Barry Fowler

Nae doot ye've herd the news. A date's bin set
fir aw as yin tae tak a leap o'faith
intae a future nain could e'er regret,
the ballot box's democratic lathe
wance an fir aw tae pit paid tae they myths
thit muckle's bonny, it laist tae brek free
fae Whiteha's faur-flung monoliths,
gie awbody the right t' equality
insteed o' wars, injustice, wanton greed,
no restin till we see aw nuclear missiles
replaced wi nature's bombs, bricht pollen seed
blawn frae the flowery croons o' glorious thistles,
showin oor world neebors thit we're in guid fettle.
Aye, noo's the oor tae grab haud o' the nettle.

The Universe Celebrates the New Dawn

Alan Gay

Dressed to kill in velvet lit with sequins
the constellations lay out their best crystal
you can almost hear the Seven Sisters clink their glasses
the Milky Way bubbles and pops like champagne
stars hang on chandeliers

Meteors grant wishes in a display of early fireworks
Polaris winks down on upturned heads
The Great Bear, that old swinger,
catches lightning bolts in its paws
Orion himself stands wide-legged in applause

The whole firmament draws breath to shout, clap
wave its hat at the first hint of rising sun
when a brass gong will resound long
into the blackcloth stars which in their brightness stun

A Questionnaire for Citizens of an Independent Scotland

Harry Giles

Are you thrilled by excellence?
Are you always curious about the world?
Are you thrilled when you learn something new?
Can you bend to touch your knees and straighten up again?
Are most of your friends more imaginative than you?
What is the Enlightment?
Can you use a pen or pencil?
Can you undo blouse buttons?
Can you recognise a friend?
Where does Father Christmas come from?

Do you have trouble accepting love from others?
Can your speech be understood by strangers?
Are you any good at planning group activities?
Are you able to fit in, no matter what the social situation?
Do you ever say funny things?
Do you mope a lot?
Do pain and disappointment often get the better of you?
Do you have control over the voiding of the bladder?
Does your life have a strong purpose?
Do you have a calling in life?
Who is the heir to the throne?

Who defeated the Vikings?
Is the police force a public service that helps and protects?
What are the fundamental principles of Scottish life?
Do you like to think of new ways to do things?
Is it a criminal offence to carry a weapon of any kind?
Are you able to look at things and see the big picture?
Do you need verbal instruction?
Do you have a well thought-out plan for what you want to do?
How many pence are in the pound?
Can you see at all?
Can you let bygones be bygones?
Do you always try to get even?
Do you always finish what you start?

Wound

George Gunn

Take this wound that I offer you
keep it close & love it well
for the storm may run at Faraid
the surf turn white Loch Eriboll
but no wind can blow an organised people
across the unknowable ocean
or drown their history in the swell

we are cut & yes we bleed
but we are time & headland & will heal
forging our strength by Naver & Torrisdale
tempering our own steel for our own knife

so drink from this cup
the sea on your lip will tingle
the vast democracy of life

My New Homeland

Iyad Hayatleh

To my beloved wife Lamees, born 1963 in Syria, died 2013 in Glasgow

Translated by Tessa Ransford with the poet

Just a heartbeat far, it is as if I see my dream
just a character length or even closer
I see it come true
so after a while
this country will cross towards her desired horizons
with all her womanhood

And I am staying up waiting to baptise what remains of life
    in me
in her new breathing
and to witness how the dew will return to those ancient
    mornings
stormed by dark nights on their mountains
and how a shy sun will paint a new day for a new brave
    heart
as the haar on North Sea shores slowly vanishes
where thistles will rise up again from behind the mist after
    a long slumber
and I send my soul wandering like clouds of love with
    seagulls
over rivers banks
that wiped away my tears a decade and a half ago

I fly to the middle of the sky, and alight on the threshold of
      a country
in whose bosom I sought refuge, when wide deserts became
too narrow for my naive dreams
I cried and shared my sorrow with her
then loosened my deep grief on her warm shoulders
She settled me down and consoled me like a lover,
day and night
autumn, winter, spring and summer

That former country which has never been mine is burning
      my sails
destroying my boats in the madness of her chaotic sea today
and breaking the oars that I carved out of my bones for the
      love of her
She blows up my past days
and memories I sustained with tears
and cuts off the last thread that tugs an exiled stranger
to the familiarity of her cold alleys
and denies me the escape of nostalgia

That country mislaid me as child, threw me away
to the end of the earth, while a man
miles away from Galilee
waves and waves from the shores of Haifa

I arrived in the land of tales and gales
the land that never reproved my failed beginnings
the land that opened her heart like a threshing-floor
for the wheat of my poems
and sprouted in her soil the plants of my tenderness
the soil where my roses bloomed to the tune of their bagpipes
when I was a child in the refugee camp

With the twin of my soul, I came here seeking sanctuary
for us birds with broken wings
Like two swallows we landed on an arm of a pine tree
and engraved our joined soul on her skin

With two roses in our garden the country of clouds
granted us a third promising one
In the bounty of her rainfall we grew up together,
and the heather blossomed within us

The country that lit my candles in her sky among shiny stars
that took parts of myself, my Lamees and her unlimited
    dreams
in the arms of her soil
the country that made me laugh cried long
for my Lamees and for me

Today, this country presents her heart
and the keys of her ambiguous secrets to me
on a dish of delight
and with all her splendour she paves a path of hope for me,
    for all strangers

To my new homeland, whose love overwhelmed me with
    ecstasy
like dervishes in a corner of a mystery of a myth,
I chant
halleluiah, halleluiah
This land is no longer an exile

بِلادي الجديدة

إلى زوجتي الحبيبة لميس المولودة في سوريا 1963، المتوفّاة في سكوتلندا 2013

عَلى بُعدِ خَفقةِ قلبٍ، كأنّي أرى حُلُمي قابَ حَرفٍ وأدنى
فَعمّا قليلٍ، سَتَعبرُ هذي البِلادُ بِكلِّ أنوثَتِها نَحو آفاقِها المُشتهاةِ

وَها أَنَذا ساهرٌ كَي أَعَمّدَ ما ظَلّ بي مِن حياةٍ بِأنفاسِها البِكرِ
ها يُعيدُ الندى لِلجبالِ التي داهَمتها الليالي صَباحاتِها الغابِراتِ
وَترسمُ شَمسٌ خَجولٌ نَهاراً جَديداً لِقلبٍ شُجاعٍ جَديدٍ
ضَبابُ شَواطئ بحر الشمال يَنشِفُ رويداً رويداً
فَتبزغُ خَلفَ السديم أزاهيرُهُ بَعدَ طولِ سُباتٍ
وَيبعثُ روحي تَهيمُ سَحائبَ عِشقٍ مَع النورساتِ
على ضفّتي أذهرٍ كَفكفتْ قبلَ عقرٍ وَنصفٍ دموعي

أُحلّقُ حتّى حدودَ السماءِ، أحطُّ على شُرفةٍ مِن بِلادٍ
شَريداً لَجأتُ إلى صَدرِها حين ضاقَتْ بِأحلامي السانجاتِ صُدورُ الصحاري الوِساعِ
بَكيتُ، وَقاسَمتها وَحشَتي
ثُمّ أرخيتُ أحمالَ حزني الدفينِ عَلى بَحرِ أكتافِها الدافِئاتِ
بِأحضانها أسكَنتني، نَهاراً وَليلاً بِأنسِ طيورِ الهوى نادَمتني
خَريفاً، شِتاءً، رَبيعاً، وَصيفا

بِلادي التي لَم تَكُن لي
التي تُحرقُ الآنَ أشرعَتي
وَالذي بَيننا مِن مراكبَ في بَحرها الفوضويِّ الجنون
التي تَكسرُ الآنَ ما – كُنتُ يوماً – نَحتُّ لها مِن ضلوعي مَجاذيفَ وَصلٍ
وَتَنسِفُ أيّاميَ السالِفاتِ، وَذاكرةً كُنتُ حَصّنتُها بالدموع
تُمزّقُ آخرَ خيطٍ يَشدُّ الغريبَ لِدفْءِ أزقّتِها البارِداتِ
وَتَحرمني مِن حَنيني

بِلادي التي ضَيّعتني صغيراً
كَبيراً رَمتني إلى آخرِ الأرضِ
أميالَ أميالَ عن عالياتِ الجليلِ، وأمواجَ أمواجَ عن شَطٍّ حَيفا

وَصلتُ بلادَ الحكاياتِ والريح
هذي البلادُ التي– مَرّةً – ما استثارت بداياتي الخائباتِ
التي فتحت قَلبها الرحبَ بَيذَر حُبٌّ لِقمح قصيدي
التي أنبتثُ في ثَراها سَنابلَ وَجدي
وأزهرَ وَردي على دَندناتِ مزاميرها مِن زمانِ المخيّم

جِئتُ وَتوأمةُ الروحِ نَسألُها مَلجأً للطيورِ التي هِيضَ جُنحائها وَاستُبيحَتْ
كَطيري سُنونو بُعَيدَ اغترابٍ طَويلٍ حَطَطنا على راحة السنديانِ
نَقَشنا على خَدّ أغصانِها روحَنا الواحدةُ
وكان بِبستاننا وردتينِ، بلادُ الغيوم حَبتنا بِثالثةٍ واعدةٌ
كَبِرنا سويّاً، وَفتَح فينا وَمِنّا الخَلَنجُ على خيرِ أمطارِها

البلادُ التي أوقدت في سَماها مَع الأنجُمِ الساهراتِ شموعي
وضَمّت بأحضانِ تُربتِها بَعضَ نفسي، لَميسي وأحلامها الباسقاتِ
البلادُ التي أضحكَتني، بكّتها طويلاً، وأيضاً بَكّتني
عَلى طَبَقٍ مِن وِدادٍ هيَ اليومَ تَمنحُني قَلبَها، مَفاتيحَ أسرارِها الغامِضاتِ
وَترصفُ بالحبّ لي، لِلغريبينَ في أَلَقٍ دَربَها
هَللويا .. هَللويا
وإنّي لأرضِي الجديدةِ، مِثلَ دراويشٍ زاويةٍ في خَبايا الحكايا أغنّي
وَيُسكِرُني حبُّها
لَمْ تَعد هذه الأرض منفى

إياد حياتله
شاعر فلسطيني مقيم في سكوتلاند

Aye

William Hershaw

Let go the blessed English to their shires,
Their meadows, downs, dog rose and misty turns,
Their churches, yews, flat lands and haunted spires –
Remember Wordsworth and his love for Burns.
Remember English heroes like Tom Paine,
Their honesty and fairness sorely won
Who scorned the yoke of Royalty just the same.
Then mind the ghostly twelfth man at mid-on.

For ours was aye the enemy within –
It was not the docile English forged our woe:
Our lads o pairts, our very kith and kin,
With dominies and tawses taught us No.
A Calvinist heart is thrawn to forgive –
Let it all thaw   forgive, then love and live.

Caledonian Mansions

for David Betteridge

Tom Hubbard

(At Kelvinbridge, Glasgow; designed by James Miller,
1896; built 1897)

Balustrades on balconies; oriels and curlicues,
Half-rhymes in russet stone – those turrets, domed, spired,
To upraise an unlikely Istanbul-on-Kelvin –
Close-knit labyrinth of attic and cellar, strict line, rebel curve:
Clyde-built ship, on dry land, but not too dry,
Restrained inebriation,
Architectural bevvy and no-bevvy, both!

Nothing boringly postmodern about this.
Here are homes, shops, community,
The palpabilities of things made
With the personalities of the folk making them.
That's the Scotland for us.

Not by Mackintosh – but it seems to have *grown* here,
Organically, imperceptibly – and with human sweat.
A bourgeois building? Ay, but we've got it now,
Free for the looking, admiring, venturing in,
For faláfel and samosa of the co-operative,
Or nerds (like me) among second-hand records:
Lured in by Mozart and leaving with Mussorgsky,
Lured in by Mussorgsky and leaving with Mozart.
A local bookstore with real books in it,

And staffed by those who know what they're talking about,
Who grew up here, can tell you who writes, who reads.

An ideal palace, the model
For a gentle, confident people.
That's the Scotland for us:
Discovered corridors, correspondences, integrative vision.

With a swish of his whisk, or wand

Gordon Jarvie

Remembering Deji (or chief) Olaiya Fagbamigge
(1925–1983), of Akure, Nigeria

Aged in his nineties, a chief of the town of Akure,
as lately as 1953, was still the embodiment
of a traditional way of life. That was the year

when he finally rebuffed overtures
from some Christian churches to build
a chapel within his vast palace compound.

Describing their proposals as superfluous,
he pointed out proudly that his compound already
had within its walls the temples and shrines
of seven hundred and twenty deities.

Then, with a collective swish of their wands,
the Deji's courtiers dismissed the Christians
from his chiefly presence. End of audience.

Scotland My Scotland

Anne B Murray

Scotland my Scotland, my Africa, my own land, from
Aberdeen to Ardnamurchan Point, I give you Ae Fond
Kiss.

Blackpudding for Breakfast, Burns for Supper.
Buzzards, tiny on the skyline as they chase away the eagle.

Castles and Claymores, Cathedral Cities, Clachan pubs.

Drystane Dykes, Dunces, Down-and-outs and Drunks.

Estuaries, Edinburgh, Explorers and Emigrating Engineers.

Falcon and Fieldfare, Firths and Feu duties.

Glamis, Glasgow, Gallous Grannies playing Golf.

Heather honey, Heron, Heraldry. Hill beyond Hill beyond
Hill.

Islands and Inlets, Italian Ice-cream, Irn-Bru.

Jams and Jellies and Jeely pieces. And why do they call us
Jock?

Kilts and Kerry-oots.

Lochs and Lochans, the Lion Rampant, gi'in it Laldy.

Majestic Mountains, Memorable Mists and the Misery of
Midgies, Muir, MacDiarmid, Morgan, MacCaig. And Mary,
Queen of Scots.

Nevis and Nessie and North Sea oil.

O for my Own land, On yersel' hen.
Otters and Ospreys, Oatmeal and Angus Og.

Pride. Scottish Pride – our bread and butter!
Porridge, Prebyterianism, Passing Places, Peat bogs and
Pedagogues, Patriotism, Pop groups and Paths that peter out.

Queen's views, Quality fudges.

Rain and Rain and Rousing choruses at football matches –
our support is so much stronger than our team.

Sheep, Salmon, Shenanigans and Sheltering from the Storm.
The Scott Sutherland Commando Monument *'This land
their training ground.'*

T is for Tourists, trying to get served; for Tall Tenements,
and wee Toddies for the Toothache.

Umbrellas, abandoned, broken, in the streets.

Very hot Vindaloo.

Whisky and Weather; Woolly rugs and Weather; Walkers
and Weather. Wild and Wonderful Wester Ross.

X is for xxx-ing out a few mistakes, I wish we could.
And for centres of Excellence and drinking to Excess.

Y is Yous Yins, listenin' tae this.

Zzz? Scotland my Scotland, my zareba, my Africa, my own
land – I love you.

The Mornin Eftir

Stuart McHardy

The mornin eftir
there'll be heids
like kettles crashin
een like holes
in yellae snaw
an wames like Arctic storms;
but
there'll be nae cries o
misery
jist the creakin soun
o openin doors.

Freeing the Unicorn
(in memory of Colin Macleod of Govan)

Alastair McIntosh

Have you ever wondered
why the Lion of Empire's might
stands rampant roaring proud
and not a little – loud –
while Unicorn of quiet understated way
(and therefore dangerous –
I've heard the anxious voices say)
is held in chains, tamed and restrained
from being magic, holy, wild and free
one-pointed spiral of awareness
that reaches from within this land
and on through you and me?

Macleod asked that portentous question
back in Devolution protest days
United Kindred camping out on Calton Hill ...
and girding up his loins to leap
as if a mythic beast on pounding wings
(with angle-grinder hitched onto his back)
he scaled the gates of Holyrood
with dreadlocks flying
eye of eagle, scrying

And though seen off by Palace guards
amidst the clamour of alarms, the yelp of dogs ...
and though turned back hotfooting it
across the gold-trimmed iron-cast gate
before the spinning diamond wheel could bite ...
Too late! The manacles that weighed upon
old Scotia's shoulder clattered crumpling
down onto the deadening cobbles ...
cut right through by searing blade
in realm of Spirit from within (for such is where
their deepest bondage
always lay)

That night beneath the stars high out on Arthur's Seat
sweet Finlay's People skirled their pipes and reeled
and stirred the Rhymer's slumbering clans awake –
one-pointed – gathered – to demanding common task
While shepherds watching o'er the White Stag's herd
perceived the Holy Rood, ablaze! – the compass
fire of Scotland's love (*put off thy shoes*
tread gently, child, upon this ground)
great opening of our people's way
for native, poor and also refugee

Receive this flame, this life that is
the Unicorn's God-sent decree
that reaches to the hearts of
you, and even that of me
... Magic, Holy
Wild – and
Free

Saorsa / Freedom / Fredome

for Tamim Al-Barghouti

Aonghas MacNeacail

saorsa

bhi coimhead amach air an raon mu mo choinneamh
le fios gu bheil gach glac, bruach is lian fosgailte dha
mo sheasamh, dha mo shìnteag, dha mo dhabhdail,
gur ann bhuam fhìn a tha an cead ri fhaotainn airson
sìol a chur, airson dearc a preas, airson inilteadh spréidh,
nach eil freiceadair aig oir na craite, deiseil airson mo
shèamadh, airson maoidheadh orm, airson mo shaothair
a shuaineadh,
    ach seall, air fàire, thar fàire, na tha seasamh
mu choinneamh nam balla, nan callaid, a tha gu dìon air
an càradh eadar iad fhéin agus raon farsaing am miann
an lìonmhorachd shùilean rùnach, gach cridhe lùigeach

có nach iarradh boile dearg ceann foighidinn ag éiridh
bho gach broilleach glaiste thar oir nach do dh'iarrar –
thar na h-uaill ìmpireach a dhèanadh gainntir de gach
anam, anns an glasar ar n'aignidhean neo-dheimhinne
gun shoillse eòlais, gun daras còire no uinneag dòighe

carson nach faodar leinn amas cruaidh na fìorachd, a tha
'n ar smior, a chuimseachadh air a mheàirle bhraoisgeach
a tha saoiltinn tèarainte maoin sheasgair an còmhdach
agus iadsan gléidhte ann an lùchairtean fillte ar cnàmhan

freedom

to be looking out on the landscape before me,
knowing every hollow, slope and meadow is open
to my standing there, my striding, my dawdling,
that it's from myself permission is obtained, to
plant seed, pick berry from bush, let cattle graze,
that there's no sentry at the croft's edge, ready to
prohibit me, to threaten me, to reduce my efforts
to embroilment,
    but see, on and beyond horizons, how many
stand outside the walls, the fences, that are securely
set between them and the broad field of their desires,
those innumerable longing eyes, every wishing heart

and why not allow a red rage of spent patience to arise
from each breast that's locked beyond unwanted borders –
beyond imperial vanities that would make a prison of every
soul, wherein they might lock our own unresolved minds,
with no informing light, door of justice, window of hope

why shouldn't we take reality's objective steel, that's in
our marrow, aiming at the grinning agents of brigandage
who think secure the protecting wealth that clothes them
as they take shelter in the layered palaces of our bones

fredome

tae be leukin oot at the landscape afore me
kennin ilka howe, brae an lea is appen
tae ma staundin thair, ma stendin, ma daidlin,
that it's fae masel permeesion's gotten, tae
plant seed, tak berry fae buss, lat kye girse,
thair bein nae gird at the craft's bond, ready tae
prescrive me, tae threiten me, tae skewl ma ettlins
tae raivelins,
    but see, on and ayont easins, hou mony
staund furth the waws an fences stellit siccar
atween thaimsels an the braid leas o their seekins,
thae coontless greenin ees, ilka wissin hert

an whit for no lat reid radge o exowstit thole tae hove
fae ilka briest at's lucken ayont unsocht mairches –
ayont imperial vainities at wad mak a jyle o ivery
saul, wherein thay micht lock oor ain switherin mynds,
wi nae a kythin licht, door o juistice, winnock o howp

whit for shoudna we take reality's jonick steel, at's in
oor marrae, ettlin at thae gangein factors o cateranin
wha ween siccar the hainin walth at cleids thaim
as hay take bieldin in the sclifferit pailaces o wir banes

19-9-14

Stuart A. Paterson

First light, I saw red in the sky's
Angry fanfare, fiery waterfalls
Belching through black cloud,
My upturned white face
Catching cold rays of sun,
My hands in my pockets, blue
And sore from clenching
Against thin fists of merciless wind.
Eyes streaming & looking
Over to Cumbria, caught between
Somewhere neither England
Nor Scotland, or me, I felt
For a second like a tiny
Tattered flag, battered & blown
To bits, 'til all that remained
Was a ragged hand unclenching,
Stretching out fingers to
Colour the sunrise blue.

Surge

Nalini Paul

The tide yawns in and out
 of the sea loch
 yearns and moves
  to wider expanses.

Language drowns
  like salt-rubbed tombstones.

Then sound emerges
 a waterlogged bell
  washed with the cathedral.

Our differences settle into stained glass
fragments form and image

voices sing.

We write each line of a sonnet
 in water
shaping a welcome out of clarity
 light
 chatter
 trout
 heather

Black-and-white
 passes us
  slips and fades

That monochrome way
   of seeing is gone

The husk of our remembering
   raises the sun
       and colours are born.

Untitled

Tom Pow

before independence
chopping wood, drawing water

after independence
drawing water, chopping wood

Scotland's Thistle

John Purser

Your spiked leaves drawing blood:
belligerent beauty, wounding the heart:
all to protect a proud purple crown,
that its soft thistle-down may float
in active air, on liberating winds,
to spread the urgent seed
like a free sovereign people growing.

Is there a Country?

Tessa Ransford

My soul there is a country my parents used to know
a country sore and sorry reaching for a better world
they humped coal and cleaned the grate
they queued in shops and trudged the windy street
they hoped, believed, encouraged,
were witty, kind and good.

My soul is there a country now
which they would recognise?
The way we live more comfortably
with electronic systems;
the way we mix and marry and
swop our children round;
the way we travel freely
and communicate, no waiting
for replies, no longing, searching,
as there used to be, no aching;
cars and wars still multiply
with cruelty and stupidity
as we fail to learn, despite
the information revolution,
what we need to know for real:
what makes the commonweal.

My soul there is a country you may visit in the future
when women will be happy and playgrounds will abound
when animals are understood and sharing is rewarded
when cities are for local markets
when land is allocated so that all can grow some food
when learning is provided by those with skill and reason
and stories keep us wise,
the old are not neglected and the young are not exploited,
a world of human kindness
we do know how
we know we must allow.

A Modest Proposal

Angus Reid

if I as a writer of   poetry
were called upon to give   a form of words
to model the nation's   behaviour
it would be this

ownership obliges
everyone to respect and   to care for
the sacred
to respect and   to care for
freedom of conscience

and to recognise
the gift of   *every individual*
to respect it
care for it   nourish it
to care for and protect *communities*
and
to care for *the land*
and wherever
the land has been abused to   restore it
so that it can support all forms of   life

five principles   five fingers on the hand

The Argument

Alan Riach

It was in the 1950s,
London then became
what we might call the nexus of
'metropolitan centralisation':
government, banks, the Treasury,
the BBC, the 'voice of the nation'.

No. Not this nation
The system is us. Change it.
Let it no longer be
'Business as usual.' End
the condescension.

Oh Pride, that vulnerable thing,
Oh Shame, that terrible weight.

Sunup. Daylight burning.
The mistakes you have made you will know
within three years. But now, how long
before another dawn like this will come?
It will come.

Auld Reikie

Paul Henderson Scott

For Dunbar it was the mirry toun.
Fergusson cried it a canty hole
And like a keek o glore and heaven forby.
Here Hume transformed human thocht
and gave bien denners tae his freens.
Clerk Maxwell as a bairn at schule
Scrievit a paper for the Royal Society.

For thae that hae the lugs tae hear
Thae splores, high jinks, high thochts
Still echo roon closes, wynds,
Howfs and new toun drawing rooms.
In oor ain time Garioch and Smith
Were guy sib to Fergusson himself.
The sheer beauty o the place still lifts the hert,
A beauty which some hae done their best tae hash.

For there's muckle to gar ye grue
In Auld Reikie and in aw Scotland thae days:
Puirtith, ignorance and hopelessness,
Shoddy bigins, ill health, early daith,
Amang the warst in Europe tae oor shame.
Cheek by jowl wi commercial greed,
Affluence, mobile phones and jaunts tae Bangkok,
Efter three hunner year o nae government or
    misgovernment.

But noo there's a glisk o hope.
At last we hae oor Parliament back,
Reined yet by Westminster,
But sune we'll ding thae traces doon.
Ower lang oor caws for equality and social justice
Hae fallen on deif and distant lugs.
Sune we shall bigg a new and fairer Scotland
Wi Reikie a real capital aince mair.

Alba

for Tony McManus

Donald Smith

half sunk in peat
stone grey slumber
Finn's giant sleep
in centuries wind
and weather worn
till at the whistle
matted shoulders
shrug, heave out,
a round to lumber

wake from sleep, night is passing

solitary houses
break horizon
sea walls gape,
imprints flitting
by ruined lochans
more birds flock
than people
as wild geese
home northwards

over the hills, light is showing

on city crossroads
by river quayside
long columns form
to join the ships
kitbags on shoulder
masted sail, mist
boatloads living
memory borne
the lost return

land fit to live

time wreaths
pavie and machair
flower-wearing fields
crowd together
ringing tears
into tomorrow
shadows dance
on roof tops
before rising

wake from sleep, night is passing
over the hills, light is showing
land fit to live

Head of a Young Woman
(Shetland Museum)

Gerda Stevenson

I press my brow to cold glass –
two women, head to head:
your face tilts like a ship's prow
challenging the wind,
morning sky over the North Sea
in your salt-washed cheeks
and eager, blue-green eyes.
Your hair falls like mine
from a centre parting, though holds
no trace of grey in its peat brown sweep.
Five thousand years between us, and yet
not a moment, it seems – recognition
like that spark you'd know how to strike
from stone. Thought tugs at your mouth's harbour,
a half-smile about to slip its mooring into laughter.

Your skull lies beside you, mute echo,
shell-white in spotlit stillness – every curve
and crevice mapped by expert minds:
your mask their exquisite calculation,
more real to me than any excavated bone.

Did you sleep, wake, love and weep
in the dark air of honeycomb chambers
built by shores I've only glimpsed
from plane and car – my stay too short
and anyway, my timing out of season?
I want to know you, unknown woman,
walk with you the cliffs at Silwick,
tread the paths of Scalloway, hear
your language beat the air again
with skua, scart and arctic tern,
learn your life, those days that stretched
behind your step, and (though you couldn't guess
their end would come too soon) gave you
such a fearless gaze of hope.

The Ravens o' Thingvellir

Lorna J Waite

(*Inspired by reading Noami Mitchison's 'The Land The Ravens Found' aged 12. Written in Iceland on a Scotland football away trip.*)

The ravens found me
At the furst parliament
Atween tectonic plates
A flew a Saltire hopefully
Find yer voice Scotland
Are the ravens o' the Law Rock
Whispering wurdz fae the new
Morality
Are your soldiers free?
Why dae ye kill?
Ma imagination is weary o' rid, white, blue
Murky colours plundering wi age
Staining wi war ambivalent Alba

Learn yer stories
Speak them tae the land
Listen and hear the
Water teach ye
O' waves, the flow o' imperial history
Particles o' memory minded
A smoored, tender fire hauds an ember o' heat
Unner ash warmth lingers
Let the wid mind ye o' birch, forest and
Gaelic alphabet

Let the ravens flee into yer stomach
Settle the acidic fear o' flight
I cannae stomach Empire ony mair
Clean an' cool, the clarity o' tide
Washes oot oor union
Woman blood drips oan our goodbye
withoot fears

Let us be, as it will be
A Republic of Scots
Let iz be, mar a bhitheas e
Poblachd Albannaich

Gie Peace A Chance

Brian Whittingham

On YouTube, the '60s newsreel shows a black and white
    Dunoon.
Smartly dressed Ban the Bombers.
To Hell with Polaris placards
reminding us that H stands for Hiroshima
as well as Holy Loch.

A lone folkie strums as he marches

> *Ban Polaris Hallelujah, Ban Polaris Hallelujah,*
> *Ban Polaris Hallelujah*
> *… and send the Yankees home!*

A few posters with the white Ban the Bomb symbol
on its black background.
A young well-dressed Michael Foot
behind a well-behaved pipe band.

Onlookers record the event on their Box Brownie cameras.

Fast forward fifty year.
Glasgow's George Square.
They're still marching still protesting.

This time a choir sings as they march …

> *It takes your left leg off*
> *It takes your right leg off*
> *Your eyes fall out and the dust makes you cough*

Gie Peace a Chance placards.

Drummers pound a defiant beat
to shrill piercing whistles
orchestrated by their conductor

as pavement onlookers join in
swaying to their passing rhythm.

Pre nuptial

Christie Williamson

At Partick Cross
he kent strett on
wis best. Wast
tae da last
o sun at smelt
laek lippenin sumtheen
du's ay wantit
but nivvir seen
athin dy raek.

On his airm
he wore his heart,
inked in bi needles
brunt prood bi dis haet.
Ower da kjist
o da Lion Rampant
'Scotland'. A banner
fur aathin he airnt
his airly limp fur.

Sayin Yes isna
aboot steppin awa fae
onythin or onybody
but steppin up
ta wha we ir.
So whan A'm axed
'Do you believe the people
of Scotland should govern
their own affairs?'

Naebidy better
fur da job
(an wi ir tried).
Fur richer or poorer
I do.

Veesion

Rab Wilson

Sklentin oot, ower victory's field across,
Æthelstan's airmy, routit, bate an brucken,
Nou Óengus minds his wird forenenst the veesion;
Cloods that formt the shape o Andra's cross.
That eemage stounds tae us doun throu the years,
An nou we face agane stairk, vital chyces,
Nou wir nation's fortune aiblins rises?
Daur we hae thon stieve smeddum o *his* fieres?
Rax forrit, aiblins twa, three mair decades,
An see a Scotland walthy, bien an free,
Siccar in hersel tae bear the gree,
Destiny mappit oot – it's yours tae hae,
An syne thon day wull daw tae cast yer vote,
Yer ain *crux decussata*, markit 'howp'.

In 832 AD Oengus II led his army of Picts and Scots against the
English army of Angles led by King Aethelstan. The Scots army
was victorious and this paved the way towards an independent
Scotland. Oengus famously prayed to Saint Andrew the night
before the battle and stated he would appoint Andrew as Patron
Saint of Scotland if he won. On the day of the battle, legend states
a white cross appeared in the sky above the battlefield foretelling
Oengus's victory. The day is again approaching when the Scots
people will have to decide on their country's destiny. The Saltire,
or crux decussata, comes from the Latin crux, 'cross', and decussis,
'having the shape of the Roman numeral X' – denoting the shape
of the cross Saint Andrew was crucified on.

Landfall

Donald Adamson

Everything came from somewhere else.
The land arrived as lava or by sea,
minches were shaped, tongued, grooved
in the waltz of continents,
words knocked spots off each other,
letters were hacked and notched
by Romans and Vikings,
merchants, monks and scribes.
Tribes travelled, said 'Ach well' and stayed.

And here, finding ways of being
this piece of earth
whose cities, lochs and moors
inhabit us, we are –
a motley crew.

Orkney

Ken Cockburn

we sail past Stroma's empty fields
the Maidens grind the sea-gods' salt
binoculars to scan the scene
the latent power the races hold

divers down among the wrecks
I don't know what it is I've found
a haar drifts in across the rocks
the crab's blue shell fades in the sun

the Romans came and saw and left
Vikings named themselves in runes
a hoard of shards the dig unearthed
the sacred grove is made of stone

unfurl your banner to the breeze
starlings wheel across the sky
a spotted orchid in the verge
the wind is in the blades and flags

Koan

in memoriam George Philp

Colin Donati

O U T spells oot

Choinneach at the Peats

Morgan Downie

Not what he expected to be doing, not
at his age, but what with the price of oil
we must do what we must, says Choinneach
at the peats, early in the season, before
the flies, but still the work is hard.
At least you have the skills for it I say,
and Choinneach agrees, the young
today never learned and if they did
never had the proper practice of it.

As is customary with those parted by time
we commence the talk with the dead
and follow on with misfortune. First,
the misfortune of the acquainted
and then the misfortune of those
with whom we are not. Next is talk
of lambing, of which there is much
here, and after that the barley, of which
there is not. My dry lips untroubled.

I was wondering, says Choinneach,
why it might be that here in the peatland,
as you raise your hand in greeting, your
pocket is so strangely free of a dram.
I was wondering if the *curum* had come
upon you. A question only half in jest.
God stands in the empty air between us
as he has before. This is the lay of our talk,
we two who have been long parted.

Until Choinneach sighs and places his hand
upon his idle spade. I do not take it.
It is not my custom. I, who in his eyes,
though we have shared fishing time together,
will never be better than half an islander,
with bad Gaelic. You may call me by
many names – incomer, outsider,
but, *bodach*, I cut peat for no man
that does not heat my fire alone.

Lenin Ponders Voting Yes

Alistair Findlay

We were gamblers at the feenish, Joe, miners betting on
    the edge,
the roof wid haud, weighing the odds on whose national
    bourgeoisie was best
tae back, or not, when thir struggles against imperialism,
    the foreign thief,
turned inevitably toward robbin' thir ain masses, thir
    former allies,
the proletariat, progressives tae reactionaries in yin fell
    swoop,
as the dialectic drove us tae backin' ony looney willin' tae
    support the Soviet state,
the Great Russian chauvinist, I saw, too late, emergin'
    oan my daith-bed.

The nationalism o' the oppressed sud aye be unyoked
    frae the oppressor's, I wrote,
for the nationals o' big nations are guilty o' gi'en too
    little tae thir minorities,
nivir too much, so it's been, well, liberatin', watchin'
    this gallus, raucle nation
pull the plug on Tory Britain's addled dream o' Empire,
    MacDiarmid's *leper pearl*.

Lunar Phenomenon

Alan Gay

On the night of Wednesday 17 September 2013
the Almanac records the moon hanging
in the dark half of the lunar month

The Earth's shadow
thrown by the sun onto the moon
is a shutter closing on old light
For a while a corona circles the rim –
a promise of what must follow

The moon grows day by day
as the shutter slides open

There is nothing unusual about a new moon
except that this one pours down light
stronger and bolder than seen this epoch

Shadows creep away. Silver splashes everywhere
Night turns into day

Maeshowe

Harry Giles

Lown i the lair
o five thoosan year,
we wauk the luntit
lip o winter
whiles hit sains
the runit flags.

We're suithless: gabbin,
lowsin shaidaes,
raxin for some kin o
mynt i the muivement
o starns n stanes.

Haud haunds n braith.
Aw unconcernit
the thief cried sun
steals intae the rouk.

The wicht cried muin
taks back the lift.
Wi sou wi the birlin.

Banes wir niver
kistit here.

Nae faith but in time.

Wren
for Karine Polwart

George Gunn

This is the poem in which a wren
will change the world
read on
if there is nothing
after this
then the world
will have changed

the headland is still there
the waves still break on the shore
but look
the wren flies in through the back door
& shuts it against hunger
see how the front door
is opened to the poor

The Sea Maw

William Hershaw

The Canongait Kirkyaird – turn o the year:
The oubit DNA o Adam Smith
Unraiveling whaur wee rosiers are bare;
Fergusson mells i the cley underfuit.
Some minger gaun ben has cowped a fish supper,
Disposable chips. A sea maw fleps and lauchs:
'The food o the Gods and aiblins Alf Tupper!
Finders keepers, first dibs ma fiers, – piss aff!'
Economic migrant inben fae Gullane,
Saut days o puirtith thonder forgotten:
Why screigh aa day for bonnie caller herrin?
There's rowth o broun sauce here for fethered rottans!
He steeks his gub wi greasy battered crumbs –
Sea buirds as weill mak wales, haud referendums.

An African artefact fetches up at St Andrews

Gordon Jarvie

Sat in museum high and dry by a grey North Sea
these tropic artefacts are hard to understand –
flotsam stranded along the West Sands
of a wintry northern European coastline.

The donor called his exhibit a witch doctor's wand.
Fair enough. Nowadays we might name it a symbol
of ceremonial empowerment, badge
of a wise man's heft within his village.

He'd use it when dancing to placate the spirits
of water, of fertility, of the forest (or whatever)
by entertaining them. In tribal cultures, dance
is a sacred element, like drums, face paintings,
figurines of ancestors, staffs of office, masks,
wood carvings, ornate stools (for thrones)
and even simple whisks – as in this example.

This one's from Zambia's Toka tribe.
Similar items occur all over sub-Saharan Africa
from Ghana to Kenya, Botswana, Namibia...

The Rising of the Kelpies

(public opening, Easter 2014)

Alastair McIntosh

Now do you see the great *Each-uisge*
water horse – twin kelpies towering vaster
even than their kindred on Loch Ness
from banks betwixt the Forth and Clyde?
And rising likewise spirited
upon page one of Chapter One
– the book of *Scotland's Future*

Each-uisge – harbinger of 'doom'
and that as 'law' as *dharma*
of our destiny unfurling;
a *kairos* time, our turning point
of transformation that wells up
from lochs and rivers – even now
canals it seems – that stir and flow
and carry ships on currents deep discerned
by artists, bards and other prophets who
perceive the signs that speak unto
the shifting humours of these times

I tell you: Scotland's name
will not go down in history
for the title of our currency or
scrapping of the Bedroom Tax or
wealth of oil or even Europe
(whether in or out or round about)

Scotland's name will be a light
a healing of the nations –
the day *we set off Trident*
the day we press red button of dispatch
each one of us within the polling booth
no cruel *explosion* but a soft *implosion*
within the very politics
they thought this evil would protect

Sent back again, sent back by us
to think again –
Repent! Repent! Repent!

A! Fredome is a noble thing!
(we'll hae nae thermonuclear warheads here)
Away! Away! Away! Away!
thus speaks the great *Each-uisge* on
its Easter rising day

Latha samhraidh /
A Summer Day

Aonghas MacNeacail

latha samhraidh

chan eil nì shuas
     ach guirme
's a ghrian air an oir thall
     na seòl bàn gu pasgadh
gun ghealltainn ann
     nach till na neòil
mus tig sìolachadh air
     na dh'iarradh sinn fàs
de dh'fheur, de chàl, de
     ghàire, de dhòchas

a summer day

there's nothing above
     but blue
and the sun on the far edge
     a pale sail furling
with no promise
     that clouds won't return
before propagation shapes
     what we'd wish to grow
of grass, of kale, of
     laughter, of hope

Michael Marra

John Purser

Are you the fox that dances,
are your eyes headlamps,
that we stay rooted to the spot;
or is it that deep soft purring growl
that charms us into harmonies
no-one could rescue from an irretrievable edge
except yourself?

Gruff old magician, I would not dare
to play in any game with you,
and yet I know that,
now you've joined 'the one big thing',
you'd find a place for all of us
to dance and sing.

A Tryst

Tessa Ransford

I used to walk down the Canongate, empty and dark,
after another day at the Poetry Library
whose very existence depended on my work
however exhausted I was, drained and hungry;
but I had a tryst to keep with Scottish poetry;
and I'd compare myself to my seafaring ancestor
who sailed to Australia in a Clyde paddle-steamer.

If he overcame the dangerous currents and oceans,
attacks by pirates and running out of fuel,
I could surely sail on with minimum funds
when I had a chart, a vision and a goal
with a volunteer crew of experts, friends and faithful
navigators; like ancient Celtic adventurers
we set afloat a curragh of poetry practitioners.

Such risk in action brings its accompaniment
and gathers its own momentum and impetus.
To wait and see or slump in bewilderment
will never achieve our destiny, our bliss.
To make our own decisions and choose our course
will see us voyage ahead on a life of adventure
and find our way to what next desirable harbour?

look! – a successful Scottish colony

Angus Reid

look

a successful Scottish	C olony
like Kilda-folk standing	O n a clifftop
in a blue parliament harebells like	M en
accustomed to	M aking their own music
to making the best	O f a break in the
weather and belonging to no	N ation
on the thinness of that standing thread	H angs
a sense of purpose a song	A nd sounding
in the echo of itself it	R ings its
bell its own	E xquisite manifesto
what if the harebell had been the	B lueprint
for Darien what if that	E xample
of Scottishness were the unRoman	L aw
by which was told how to live and	L et live

John Commonweal
for Tom Fleming and Jamie Stuart

Donald Smith

Its no hauf dune, see
an aa the coort gaitheit
king, lords, fair weemen,
wi wheedlers an whingers,
an the sleekit releegious,
smooth toungit sookers up,
whan ower the waa loups
oor man johnnie, aye,
commonweal he cries hissel
an he's nae feart fur ony.

Neist he caas oot puirtith,
hunger an oppressioun
fur the king tae tak witness,
an that gies the haill
clanjamfrie the boak
tentin tae choke aa the lees
doun their daintie thrapples.

But he's nae feenished yet
oor Johnnie Commonweal
nae by hauf, nae fear,
fur guid buik in haund
he cries oan Divine
Correctioun hissel as Judge
tae sort them aa oot.

Goad kens whaur it'll wind up
wance ye stert intae thon.
Mind, no but at the last,
afore fowk turned broodie
a muckle Fule, fou gyte
oerthraws aa thrie estaitis
fur a pairliament o fules.
Aye, an us the pack o eedjits
waistin a haill holiday
oan sic clishmaclaivers.

Hame-comin

Gerda Stevenson

Hame, hame, hame on the truck,
the wheels grind their grumly air,
hame tae ma mither, ma faither, ma lass,
but I canna come hame in ma hert nae mair,
noo that ma fieres are laid in the grund,
and the desert sun has blurred ma een,
stour in ma mind frae yon cramasie flooer
that smoors aa pain on field and street,
no, I canna, canna come hame in ma hert
noo I've duin whit I've duin
(orders are orders, ye dae whit ye maun),
and I've seen whit I've seen:

oh, the bluid that brak through her skin
like a flooer frae its bud, yon bairn
that cam runnin, birlin, lauchin, skirlin
intae the faimily dance o mirth
we blew tae hell like a smirr o eldritch confetti;

and noo I'm here, hame on the truck,
ma fieres in the grund, but I canna come hame
nae mair in ma hert, for hame's naewhaur
when yer hert's deid – nae langer sair – juist deid
wi dule and the wecht o bluid fallin like flooers,
cramasie flooers, that kill aa pain, smoor yer mind,
deid, deid, as the wheels grind.

Auchencairn, and Scotland, as it Should Be

Hugh McMillan

Dick Hattaraik and Billy Marshall
are drinking at the bar.
It's blue and carved from a boat
and they are sharing some porky scratchings
smuggled over last night from Holland.
On the bay, the Black Pearl, no Prince,
rocks at anchor, carronades trained
steadily up the Dumfries road.
Outside, in a blaze of grass and yellow vetch,
some of Billy's eighty-six children
play with an exciseman's hat,
while the exciseman himself
sits blushing, winding yarn for the daughter
whose beauty like Helen of Troy's
is renowned from coast to coast.
It is June, the start of a brilliant summer,
they are breathing the air of Galloway
and it is rich in love and brandy and revolution.
Boundaries shimmer, shift like haze.
It's mathematically possible, in fact,
for Burns to come in
and put the icing on the cake.
Should I speak?
Tell my tales of a bit of baccy

smuggled in euro lorries,
the angry letters I've written to the Standard,
my hidden fear that in an independent Scotland
my pension might suffer?
Maybe not.

Contributors

DONALD ADAMSON is a poet and translator. He was born and brought up in Dumfries, but is now based in Dalbeattie. In 1995 he was awarded a Scottish Arts Council writer's bursary. He has lived in France and the Middle East, and has lectured in the universities of Helsinki and Jyväskylä, Finland, translating Finnish poems for *How to address the fog: Finnish poems 1978–2002* (Carcanet/Scottish Poetry Library, 2005). He co-founded *Markings* and has won several poetry competitions. His poem 'Fause Prophets', which in 1999 won the Herald Millennium Poetry Competition, is buried in a time capsule under the walls of the Scottish Poetry Library. He is a member of the Solway Festival Poets and has given readings in many venues.

JIM AITKEN is a poet and former English teacher who now tutors in Scottish Cultural Studies in Edinburgh. His last collection of poems was in fact a CD called Our Foolish Ways recorded and produced by First Reel Target in 2013.

PAMELA BEASANT is originally from Glasgow. She studied English at Oxford University. After working in London, she moved to Orkney, where she has lived ever since, working as a freelance writer and editor amongst other jobs, including care worker, books editor for *The Orcadian*, and currently arts officer for the local council. In 2007 she was awarded the first George Mackay Brown Writing Fellowship in Orkney, and later became chair of the organisation, which runs the Orkney Book Festival amongst other activities. Pamela has two grown-up children and lives with her husband in Stromness.

DAVID BETTERIDGE is a retired teacher and teacher trainer. He is the co-author of several books on English Language teaching. In 2002, Raymond Ross accepted a group of his 'Glasgow Poems' for publication in *Cencrastus*. These poems later grew to a book-length collection, *Granny Albyn's Complaint* (Smokestack Books, 2008). In a recent anthology that he edited, *A Rose Loupt Oot*, also published by Smokestack, he sets out to capture the spirit of the UCS work-in of

1972–3 through a selection of songs, poems, cartoons, witness statements, photographs, etc. by more than 50 contributors.

ANGUS CALDER was best known as a social and cultural historian. *The People's War: Britain, 1939–45* has been almost continuously in print since it appeared in 1969. Other substantial historical books followed, and two collections of essays about Scotland, past and present. He published throughout his adult life, won a Gregory Award in 1967, and was convenor of the committee which helped Tessa Ransford realise her vision of a Scottish Poetry Library in 1984. When he took early retirement from the Open University in Scotland in 1993, he wrote poetry more prolifically, and was published widely. His collections are *Waking in Waikato* (1997), *Colours of Grief* (2002) and *Dipa's Bowl* (2004) and *Sun Behind the Castle* (2007).

HAZEL BUCHAN CAMERON was born and brought up in Renfrewshire and now lives near Comrie in Perthshire. She is author of five poetry pamphlets including *The Currying Shop* (2007), which was joint winner of the Callum Macdonald Memorial Award in 2008. Red Squirrel Press published her collection *Finding IKEA* (2010) and will bring out a full collection in 2016. She administered the Scottish Pamphlet Poetry website for ten years and is currently Writer in Residence for the Royal Scottish Geographic Society based in Perth.

KEN COCKBURN is a poet and translator based in Edinburgh. His recent publication include *On the Flyleaf* (2007), *Ink* with artists in the fields (2011), and *Snapdragon*, translations of poems by Arne Rautenberg (2012). *The Road North*, a long poem written with Alec Finlay which 'translates' Basho's *Oku-no-hosomichi* (*Back Roads to Far Towns*) from 17th century Japan to contemporary Scotland, is published in autumn 2014. He is currently working (again with Finlay) *on there were our own there were the others*, a series of installations and commemorative walks at National Trust properties in England and Wales to mark the centenary of the outbreak of the First World War. www.kencockburn.co.uk

DES DILLON was born and brought up in Coatbridge. He is a poet, short story writer, novelist and dramatist writing for radio, stage, television and film. He was writer in residence at Castlemilk from 1998 to 2000, and has worked as a teacher of English, a creative writing tutor, and a TV scriptwriter. He has published two books of poetry, *Picking Brambles* (2003) and *Scunnered* (2011), and his novels have been translated into Russian and Italian. His novel, *Me and Ma Gal*, first published in 1995, was selected as one of The List/Scottish Book Trust's 100 Best Scottish Books of all time. His acclaimed play *Singin' I'm No a Billy, He's a Tim* is probably the most performed play in Scotland in the last decade. He now lives in Galloway.

COLIN DONATI is a poet, artist, musician and translator. He has edited *Playing Scotland's Story* (Luath, 2013), the first major collection of the plays of Robert McLellan (1907-85). His poetry is widely published in magazines and anthologies, was translated into French in *Huit Poètes Écossais Contemporains* (L'Harmattan, 2005), and includes the pamphlet collections *Rock is Water*, or *A History of the Theories of Rain* (Kettillonia, 2003) and *Ancient and Now* (Red Squirrel, 2010). As guitarist and vocalist he performs in the duo 'Various Moons' with cellist Robin Mason with whom he first collaborated in devising and creating the Benchtours musical theatre show, *Yellow House*, in 2007. Extracts from his Scots translation of Fyodor Dostoevsky's *Crime and Punishment* have appeared to date in *The Smoky Smirr o Rain* (Itchy Coo, 2003), *Chapman* (2012), *DIN* (forthcoming) and *Quaich: An Anthology of Translation in Scotland Today* (Evertype, 2014). He was a Hawthornden Fellow in 2011 and is a past chair of the Robert Henryson Society. A recorded collection of his songs and song-settings, *No Green Bottle*, also featuring cello by Robin Mason, will be available from August 2014.

MORGAN DOWNIE is an unreliable narrator with a deep mistrust of artist's statements. He believes in the notion that at least one out of every six statements should be wilfully untrue. His is a chequered past involving poetry, short story writing, visual, installation and textile art, book making, sculpture and all points in between. He has been widely anthologised for both short story and poetry. Until recently his artwork could only be bought on the island of Fårö. It is this connection that prompted his long-worked-upon secret history of Ingmar Bergman. When asked where he comes from, he describes a place he knows as the mythic archipelago of Scotia. Morgan Downie is an island man. He loves the bicycle and everything associated with it. He believes that all art may be contained in a single decent bike ride. Morgan Downie has always been on the road to Meikle Seggie.

ALISTAIR FINDLAY has written four previous collections of poetry, *Sex, Death and Football* (2003), *The Love Songs of John Knox* (2006), *Dancing with Big Eunice* (2010) and *Never Mind the Captions* (2011), and edited *100 Favourite Scottish Football Poems* (2007). He is also the author of *Shale Voices* (1999), a creative memoir of the shale oil communities of West Lothian. Findlay has had a diverse career, from young professional footballer to clay miner to social worker. He retired from social work in February 2009 and lives in Bathgate. He has recently taken up songwriting and supplied the lyrics for 'When the Call Comes' on the CD *No Pasaran! Scots in the Spanish Civil War*, Greentrax Records, 2012.

BARRY FOWLER is an Edinburgh poet who has been published in various literary magazines, collections and pamphlets over the past 30 years.

ALAN GAY studied Political Science and was formerly an educational advisor. He now lectures in Navigation and Meteorology and spends his summers with his wife Jancis sailing their yacht. His poetry is well placed in competitions, magazines and anthologies. His poetry pamphlets include *Songs of Sorrow* (*Conquest of the Aztecs*) (Bullseye, 2003), *Gone Sailing* (Bullseye, 2002), *All Points North* (*The Voyage to Bear Island, Spitsbergen and Greenland*) (MH Projects, 1996) and *The Boy Who Came Ashore* (Dreadful Night Press, 2006). He lives with his family in East Lothian.

HARRY GILES grew up in Orkney and is now based in Edinburgh, where he works as a poet, producer and performance artist. He holds an MA in Theatre Directing from East 15 Acting School, and in 2010 he founded the spoken word events series Inky Fingers. Harry's pamphlets *Visa Wedding* (2012) and *Oam* (2013) were published by

Stewed Rhubarb Press. In 2008 he won the National Student Slam, and in 2009 the BBC Scotland Slam. He was nominated for the London Zoo Award for Best Performance by a UK Poet in 2011, and the following year he won the national IdeasTap Poetry Competition and was shortlisted for the Scottish Book Trust New Writers Award. He was the Govanhill Baths Artist-in-Residence 2013.

GEORGE GUNN was born in Caithness where he returned to live in the mid-1990s. His latest book of poetry *A Northerly Land* was published in 2013 by Braevalla. *The Province of the Cat*, a prose book about Caithness, will be published by The Islands Book Trust in 2015. He founded Grey Coast Theatre Company in 1992 and with them has produced many plays and educational projects. In the 1970s and '80s he worked in the fishing industry and in the North Sea oil industry and his first play on that theme, *Roughneck*, was performed at the Traverse Theatre, Edinburgh in 1984. He has written over 20 stage plays, plays for BBC Radio Scotland and Radio 4, for who he has also written and presented several series such as *Coastlines* and *Islands*. He tutors in Creative Writing at The North Highland College – University of the Highlands and Islands. He lives in Thurso with his wife Christine Gunn.

IYAD HAYATLEH is a Palestinian poet and translator who was born and grew up in Syria. He has lived in Glasgow since 2000, and has taken part in many events including translation and poetry workshops. He has given many readings nationwide including at the Edinburgh International Book Festival, and published some of his poems in magazines and collective poetry books in Scotland in both languages, Arabic and English. His first collection was published by Survivor's Press in 2007, called *Beyond all Measure*. He has collaborated with poet Tessa Ransford, on a two-way translation project for a book, *Rug of a Thousand Colours*, with poems inspired by the Five Pillars of Islam, published by Luath Press in September 2012.

WILLIAM HERSHAW was born in 1957 in Newport on Tay. Both sides of the family had a coal-mining background, although his father joined the Fire Brigade. Hershaw is now Principal Teacher in English at Beath High School. The poem 'Cowdenbeath Man', which featured on the Scottish Poetry Library's Poetry Map of Scotland, describes his upbringing in Cowdenbeath, and is unusual for this poet as he usually writes in Scots. It was the title poem of the collection published by Scottish Cultural Press in 1997. In 2003 he won the Callum Macdonald Memorial Prize for his pamphlet *Winter Song*, and in 2011, first prize in the McCash Scots Poetry Competition.

TOM HUBBARD has been a Visiting Professor at the Universities of Budapest, Connecticut and Grenoble. He was the first Librarian of the Scottish Poetry Library. His novel *Marie B.* (Ravenscraig Press, 2008), is based on the life of the painter Marie Bashkirtseff. Recent poetry collections are *The Chagall Winnocks* (2011) and *Parapets and Labyrinths* (2013), both from Grace Note Publications, and *The Nyaff* (2012), from Windfall Books. He has edited a volume of essays, *The Poetry of Baudelaire* (New York: Grey House), and his second novel, *The Lucky Charm of Major Bessop*, 'a grotesque mystery of Fife', appeared from Grace Note in 2014.

GORDON JARVIE began his career as an English teacher, later working as a publisher and writer. His books include the *Bloomsbury Grammar Guide* (2nd edn 2007) and other language titles; *Scottish Folk and Fairy Tales* (2nd edn 2007); and *The Scottish Reciter*. He has edited various other anthologies, and with his wife he has written several *Scottie Books* for children. His most recent poetry collection *A Man Passing Through: Memoir with Poems Selected and New* (2014) is published by Greenwich Exchange. He lives in the East Neuk of Fife.

AONGHAS MacNEACAIL is an award-winning poet in Gaelic, English and Scots, songwriter in both folk and classical idioms, journalist, broadcaster, translator and occasional actor. He is a seasoned creative-writing workshopper with both schools and adult groups. Poetry has taken him to North America, Japan, Rome, Jerusalem, Berlin, Vienna, Warsaw, St Petersburg, the Arctic Circle, and Ireland frequently, among other international destinations. Collections include *An Seachnadh* ('The Avoiding'), *Oideachadh Ceart* ('A Proper Schooling'), *Laoidh an Donais Oig* ('Hymn to a Young

Demon') and *Rock and Water* (poems in English). His new and
selected Gaelic poems, *Deanamh Gàire ris a Chleoc* ('Laughing at
the Clock'), and a pamphlet of poems in Scots, *Ayont the Dyke*
appeared last year. A new collection of poems in English in
preparation. His song lyrics have been set to music by some of
Scotland's leading composers and recorded by many wonderful
singers. A collection of his songs should also appear soon.

STUART MCHARDY is a writer, musician, folklorist, storyteller and
poet, and has lectured on many aspects of Scottish history and
culture both in Scotland and abroad. Combining the roles of scholar
and performer gives McHardy an unusually clear insight into
tradition. As happy singing old ballads as analysing ancient legends,
he has held such posts as Director of the Scots Language Resource
Centre and President of the Pictish Arts Society. McHardy is a
prolific author, and has had several books published, including *Tales
of the Picts, Tales of Edinburgh Castle, The Quest for the Nine
Maidens, On the Trail of Scotland's Myths and Legends* and
Edinburgh and Leith Pub Guide. McHardy lives in Edinburgh with
his wife Sandra.

ALASTAIR MCINTOSH is from the Isle of Lewis and lives in Govan as a
director the GalGael Trust, founded by the late Colin Macleod. A
veteran of the Eigg land reform and Harris superquarry campaigns,
he works with liberation theology and holds fellowships at the
Centre for Human Ecology, the University of Glasgow and
Edinburgh University's School of Divinity. His books include *Soil
and Soul, Hell and High Water,* and poetry, *Love and Revolution*
(published by Luath).

HUGH MCMILLAN lives in Penpont in Dumfries and Galloway. He is a
poetry and short story writer. He was the winner in the Smith
Doorstep Poetry Competition in 2005, won the Callum Macdonald
Memorial Award in 2008, was a winner in the Cardiff International
Poetry Competition as well as being shortlisted for the Bridport Prize
and the Michael Marks Award in 2010. He has been the recipient of
five Arts Council or Creative Scotland Bursaries. He has been been
published, anthologised and broadcast widely. He is a good reader of

his work and has in the last few years read to sell-out audiences in the Wigtown, Stanza and Alberta Poetry Festivals. His new poetry collection *The Other Creatures in the Wood* has recently been published by Mariscat and he is currently working on the Wigtown Book Festival's first ever publishing commission, on contemporary visions of Dumfries and Galloway.

ANNE B MURRAY was born in Glasgow and has worked there for the past ten years as a tutor/facilitator in creative writing for Glasgow Life, a community-based adult learning project. Her pamphlet *Galilee to Gallicantu* was shortlisted for the Callum Macdonald Memorial Award 2010. Her poetry has been published in various journals including *New Writing Scotland, Cutting Teeth, Poetry Now,* and in *The Herald.*

STUART A. PATERSON was born in 1966 and brought up in Ayrshire in a Scots-speaking family. He was writer-in-residence for Dumfries and Galloway from 1996 to 1998, before moving to Manchester to work in the third sector for 14 years. He returned to Scotland in 2012 to live by the Solway Coast. A pamphlet, *Mulaney of Larne and other poems* was published by the University of Leiden (The Netherlands) in 1991 as part of their Scottish Poets series. His first full collection, *Saving Graces*, was published by Diehard in 1997 and shortlisted for a Saltire Society First Book Award. In 1992 he was awarded an Eric Gregory Award by the UK Society of Authors. He's had work widely anthologised and included in many reviews and newspapers in the UK and abroad, including the title poem of *Dream State: The New Scottish Poets* (Polygon) and *A Year In Poetry* (Random House), both of which featured poems describing his hopes for a future independent Scotland. In 2014, Stuart was awarded a Robert Louis Stevenson Fellowship by the Scottish Book Trust. He'll be voting AYE.

NALINI PAUL was born in India and raised in Vancouver. She moved to Scotland in 1994. At the Universities of Edinburgh and Glasgow, she studied Philosophy and English Literature, Creative Writing, and undertook a PhD on the West Indian writer, Jean Rhys. Nalini has collaborated across various art forms, including stage and film. She spent a year in Orkney as the George Mackay Brown Writing Fellow, which inspired her 2010 collection *Slokt by Sea* (Red Squirrel Press). Her pamphlet, *Skirlags* was shortlisted for the Callum Macdonald Memorial Award in 2010. Nalini's illustrated poem, Hrafn Floki, was purchased by the National Gallery of Modern Art, Special Books collection in 2014. She teaches Creative Writing in Edinburgh and Glasgow (www.whwn.co.uk).

TOM POW was born in 1950 in Edinburgh. He studied at the University of St Andrews, then taught for a number of years in Edinburgh, London and Madrid before settling in Dumfries in south west Scotland. Four of his five full collections – *Rough Seas*, *The Moth Trap*, *Landscapes and Legacies* and *Dear Alice*: *Narratives of Madness* – have won Scottish Arts Council Book Awards. As a writer for children, he won a further Scottish Arts Council Book Award. He has also written a travel book, *In the Palace of Serpents: An Experience of Peru*, and three radio plays. He was holder of the Scottish Canadian Fellowship in 1992. In 2000 he became Scotland's first Virtual Writer in Residence for the Scottish Library Association and between 2001 and 2003 was the first Writer in Residence at the Edinburgh International Book Festival. He received a Creative Scotland Award from the Scottish Arts Council in 2007 for a project exploring dying villages throughout Europe. *In The Becoming: New and Selected Poems* was published in 2009. *A Wild Adventure* – Thomas Watling, Dumfries Convict Artist – was published this year.

JOHN PURSER is well known as a composer, writer, broadcaster and musicologist. He has published three books of poetry and his poems have appeared in many magazines and anthologies. His new and collected poems *There Is No Night* is due out later this year with Zeticula Press. Of his six radio plays commissioned by the BBC, *Carver* won a Giles Cooper Award and a New York International Radio Festival Gold Medal in 1991. *Carver* was published by Methuen. In 1992 his book *Scotland's Music* won him the McVitie Scottish Writer of the Year Award. An expanded edition of *Scotland's Music* was published by Mainstream in 2007 to accompany his second eponymous radio series for BBC Scotland. In 2013 Purser brought out three CDs of his own music which have been critically acclaimed here and in the USA. Purser is a Researcher and Lecturer at Sabhal Mòr Ostaig, the Gaelic College on the Island of Skye, where he lives and crofts with his American wife, Barbara.

TESSA RANSFORD has been an established poet, translator, literary editor, essayist, reviewer and cultural activist on many fronts over the last 40 years, having also worked as founder and director of the Scottish Poetry Library. Tessa initiated the annual Callum Macdonald Memorial Award for publishers of pamphlet poetry in Scotland, now in its 14th year, with the attendant fairs and website: www.scottish-pamphlet-poetry.com. She has had Royal Literary Fund fellowships at the Centre for Human Ecology and Queen Margaret University. Tessa was president of Scottish PEN from 2003 to 2006. Tessa's *Not Just Moonshine, New and Selected Poems* was published in 2008 by Luath Press, Edinburgh. Two recent books from Luath in 2012 are a two-way translation book of poems with Palestinian poet Iyad Hayatleh, who lives in Glasgow, inspired by the Five Pillars of Islam: *Rug of a thousand colours*; and *Don't Mention this to anyone,* poems featuring India and Pakistan with Urdu calligraphy by Jila Peacock. Published most recently is a book of poems (and photographs by Michael Knowles) inspired by Edinburgh's Holyrood Park and Arthur's Seat, entitled *Made in Edinburgh.*

ANGUS REID is an independent artist. His films include *Brotherly Love, The Ring* (Best Central European Documentary Feature 2004) and *Primary School Musical!* His books include three collections of poetry: *The Gift, White Medicine* and *The Book of Days,* and *A Modest Proposal: For the Agreement of the People.* He lives and works in Edinburgh. www.angusreid.co.uk

ALAN RIACH was born in Airdrie in 1957. He studied English literature at Cambridge University from 1976–79. He completed his PhD in the Department of Scottish Literature at Glasgow University in 1986. His academic career has included positions as a post-doctoral research fellow, senior lecturer, Associate Professor and Pro-Dean in the Faculty of Arts, University of Waikato, Hamilton, New Zealand 1986–2000. He returned to Scotland in January 2001 and is currently the Professor of Scottish Literature at the University of Glasgow. His poems are collected in *This Folding Map* (1990), *An Open Return* (1991), *First & Last Songs* (1995), *Clearances* (2001) and *Homecoming* (2009). He is the co-author with Alexander Moffat of *Arts of Resistance* (2009) and *Arts of Independence* (2014).

PAUL HENDERSON SCOTT was born in Edinburgh and educated at the Royal High School and Edinburgh University. He was in 52nd (Lowland) and 7th Armed Divisions during the war and then joined the Diplomatic Service. He was in Berlin during the whole of the Soviet blockade and in Cuba during the Missile Crisis. In 1980 he returned to Edinburgh. Since then he has been Rector of Dundee University, President of both the Saltire Society and Scottish PEN, and Vice-President of the SNP and its Spokesman on Culture and International Affairs, as well as writing more than a dozen books and editing another dozen or so. His books include: *Walter Scott and Scotland, John Galt, Towards Independence, Andrew Fletcher and the Treaty of Union, Still in Bed with an Elephant, Defoe in Edinburgh and Other Papers, The Boasted Advantages, A 20th Century Life* (his autobiography), *The New Scotland*, (its sequel), *Scotland Resurgent, The Union of 1707: Why and How, The Age of Liberation* and *Scotland: A Creative Past, An Independent Future.*

DONALD SMITH is a storyteller, poet and dramatist who founded the Scottish Storytelling Centre in Edinburgh's Royal Mile. He has written widely on Scottish history and culture including a trilogy of novels exploring crisis points in Scottish society – *The English Spy, Between Ourselves* and *Ballad of the Five Marys*. His book *Storytelling Scotland: A Nation in Narrative* marked the devolution moment while his *Freedom and Faith* is a wide-ranging contribution to the Independence debate. His first poetry collection was *A Long Stride Shortens the Road: Poems of Scotland* (2004).

GERDA STEVENSON – actor, writer, director, singer/songwriter, won a Scottish BAFTA for her performance in Margaret Tait's feature film *Blue Black Permanent*. She has written plays for radio and theatre, and her poetry and prose have been widely published throughout

Britain and abroad. In 2008 she was awarded a Scottish Arts Council writer's bursary. Her play *Federer versus Murray* (shortlisted for the London Fringe Theatre Writing Award, 2010, and runner-up for the Best Scottish Contribution to Drama on the Edinburgh Fringe 2011), toured to New York in 2012, and was published there by *Salmagundi*. In 2013, her poetry collection *If This Were Real* was published by Smokestack Books, her radio drama *Homeless* was broadcast by BBC, and she was winner of the YES Arts Festival Poetry Challenge. In 2014, her play *Skeleton Wumman* was co-produced by Oran Mor, the Traverse and West Yorkshire Playhouse, and she recorded *Night Touches Day*, an album of her own songs, supported by Creative Scotland. www.gerdastevenson.co.uk

DR LORNA J. WAITE is an Edinburgh-based writer originally from Kilbirnie in Ayrshire. She was awarded her PhD 'Cultural Retrieval, Land Use and Post-Industrial Folk Memory; a practice-based response to the destruction of Glengarnock Steelworks' from the University of Dundee in 2011. She is currently Honorary Research Fellow at the University of Dundee. Her first collection of poetry, *The Steel Garden*, was published by Word Power in 2012 and she is an editor of the recently published *Rethinking Highland Art: The Visual Significance of Gaelic Culture/Sealladh às ùr air Ealain na Gàidhealtachd: Brìgh Lèirsinn ann an Dualchas nan Gàidheal*. She is a Gaelic learner and has been a lifelong supporter of Scottish independence.

BRIAN WHITTINGHAM, born and living in Glasgow, is a poet, playwright, fiction writer, editor and creative writing tutor. In 1994 he was awarded the Yaddo residency, and in 2000 he won first prize in the *Sunday Herald* Short Story Competition. His poems and stories have been widely published in anthologies and magazines. A former steelworker/draughtsman, he performed his steel-working poems as part of the BBC's *Ballad of the Big Ships* Live in Glasgow's Royal Concert Hall in 2007. He has performed and lectured in the UK, Europe and the USA, in places as diverse as beaches, universities, prisons, pubs, schools and colleges. He is currently a lecturer in creative writing at City of Glasgow College and was a visiting professor at Seattle University in 2011. His books include *Drink the*

Green Fairy, Septimus Pitt and the Grumbleoids and *Clocking In, Clocking Out: Poems on the Subject of Work*.

CHRISTIE WILLIAMSON was born in the drought summer of 1976, to the West Sandwick manse in Yell. At six years old, Christie moved to Mid Yell where he attended school, before he went to the Anderson High School in Lerwick in 1990. He enjoyed an honours degree in Film and Media Studies at the University of Stirling between 1994 and 1998, coming back in 1999 to do a Masters degree in Investment Analysis. He has lived in Glasgow since 2002, and is the proud father of two little children who are growing into big children with alarming rapidity. His first poetry collection *Oo an Feddirs* will be published by Luath in 2014.

RAB WILSON was born in New Cumnock, Ayrshire in 1960. After an engineering apprenticeship with the National Coal Board he left the pits following the miner's strike of 1984–5 to become a psychiatric nurse. As a Scots poet, his work appears regularly in *The Herald* as well as *Chapman, Lallans* and *Markings* magazines. Rab has performed his work at the Edinburgh Festival, the StAnza poetry festival at St Andrews, the Burns an' a' That Festival at Ayr and has been 'Bard of the Festival' at Wigtown, Scotland's National Book-town. Additionally Rab is a previous winner of the McCash Poetry Prize and was recently 'Robert Burns Writing Fellow – In Reading Scots' for Dumfries and Galloway Region. Currently a member of the National Committee for the Scots Language Resource Centre, Rab's list of publications includes: *Accent o the mind: Poems, chiefly in the Scots language* (2006), *Life Sentence: More Poems Chiefly in the Scots Language* (2009), *A Map for the Blind: Poems Chiefly in the Scots Language* (2011) and *Burnsiana* (2013), with Calum Colvin.

Some other books published by **LUATH** PRESS

100 Favourite Scottish Love Poems

Edited by Stewart Conn
ISBN 1 906307 66 0 PBK £7.99

In this collection, Stewart Conn mines Scotland's rich seam of love poetry in its different tongues – from traditional ballads, Burns and Scott to MacCaig, MacLean, Morgan and the vitality of Liz Lochhead and Jackie Kay; from 'Barbara Allan', 'The Blythesome Bridal' and 'Lassie Lie Near Me' to 'Hot Chick', 'Yeah Yeah Yeah' and 'Out with my Loves on a Windy Day'.

100 Favourite Scottish Poems

Edited by Stewart Conn
ISBN 978 1905222 61 2 PBK £7.99

Scotland has a long history of producing outstanding poetry From the humblest but-and-ben to the grandest castle, the nation has a great tradition of celebration and commemoration through poetry. 100 Favourite Scottish Poems ranges from ballads to Burns and from 'Cuddle Doon' to 'The Jeelie Piece Song'. Published in association with the Scottish Poetry Library.

100 Favourite Scottish Football Poems

Edited by Alistair Findlay
ISBN 978 1906307 03 5 PBK £7.99

This collection captures the passion Scots feel about football, covering every aspect of the game, from World Cup heartbreak to one-on-ones with the goalie. Feel the thump of the tackle, the thrill of victory and the expectation of supporters. Become immersed in the emotion and personality of the game as these poems reflect human experience in its sheer diversity of feeling and being.

100 Favourite Scottish Poems to Read Out Loud

Edited by Gordon Jarvie
ISBN 978 1 906307 01 1PBK £7.99

This collection includes many popular Scottish poems, from The Wee Cock Sparra to The Four Maries, The Wee Kirkcudbright Centipede to John Anderson My Jo; as well as poetry by Sheena Blackhall, Norman MacCaig, Jimmy Copeland, Tom Leonard and many others.

Whatever your choice, this wide-ranging selection will give you and your audience (even if it's only your mirror) hours of pleasure and enjoyment.

[this book] *brings home the dramatic and emotional potential that's latent in the beautiful game.*
THE LIST

Details of these and other books published by Luath Press can be found at: **www.luath.co.uk**

Luath Press Limited

committed to publishing well written books worth reading

LUATH PRESS takes its name from Robert Burns, whose little collie Luath (*Gael.,* swift or nimble) tripped up Jean Armour at a wedding and gave him the chance to speak to the woman who was to be his wife and the abiding love of his life. Burns called one of 'The Twa Dogs' Luath after Cuchullin's hunting dog in Ossian's *Fingal.* Luath Press was established in 1981 in the heart of Burns country, and now resides a few steps up the road from Burns' first lodgings on Edinburgh's Royal Mile.
Luath offers you distinctive writing with a hint of unexpected pleasures.

Most bookshops in the UK, the US, Canada, Australia, New Zealand and parts of Europe either carry our books in stock or can order them for you. To order direct from us, please send a £sterling cheque, postal order, international money order or your credit card details (number, address of cardholder and expiry date) to us at the address below. Please add post and packing as follows: UK – £1.00 per delivery address; overseas surface mail – £2.50 per delivery address; overseas airmail – £3.50 for the first book to each delivery address, plus £1.00 for each additional book by airmail to the same address. If your order is a gift, we will happily enclose your card or message at no extra charge.

Luath Press Limited
543/2 Castlehill
The Royal Mile
Edinburgh EH1 2ND
Scotland
Telephone: 0131 225 4326 (24 hours)
Fax: 0131 225 4324
email: sales@luath.co.uk
Website: www.luath.co.uk